HUMAN BODY
FACTS OR FIBS

KRISTIN J. RUSSO

Raintree is an imprint of Capstone Global Library Limited, a company incorporated in England and Wales having its registered office at 264 Banbury Road, Oxford, OX2 7DY – Registered company number: 6695582

www.raintree.co.uk
myorders@raintree.co.uk

Edited by Lauren Dupuis-Perez
Designed by Sara Radka
Production by Laura Manthe

ISBN 978 1 4747 5452 1
22 21 20 19 18
10 9 8 7 6 5 4 3 2 1

British Library Cataloguing in Publication Data
A full catalogue record for this book is available from the British Library.

Acknowledgements
Getty Images: arcady_31, cover (skeleton), asiseeit, 6, Blend Images RM, 17, Brand X, 18, 8, Colin Hawkins, 29, Corbis RF Stills, 16, EyeEm, 10, Image Source, 20, loops7, 14 (left), Photodisc, 7, serts, 21, Tara Moore, 15, Westend61, 13; iStockphoto: 7activestudio, 26, angellhell, 19, clubfoto, 14 (right), decade3d, 23 (top), Devrimb, 4, Eraxion, 25, GlobalP, 23 (bottom), laflor, 28, Nerthuz, 11 (bottom), back cover, Ocskaymark, 24, pixologicstudio, 22, somchaisom, 27, subman, 9, Svisio, background, cover (background), VladimirFLoyd, 12, Wavebreakmedia, 11 (top)

Graphic elements by Capstone Press and Book Buddy Media.

The publisher does not endorse products whose logos may appear on objects in images in this book.

Every effort has been made to contact copyright holders of material reproduced in this book. Any omissions will be rectified in subsequent printings if notice is given to the publisher.

All the internet addresses (URLs) given in this book were valid at the time of going to press. However, due to the dynamic nature of the internet, some addresses may have changed, or sites may have changed or ceased to exist since publication. While the author and publisher regret any inconvenience this may cause readers, no responsibility for any such changes can be accepted by either the author or the publisher.

Printed and bound in India.

CONTENTS

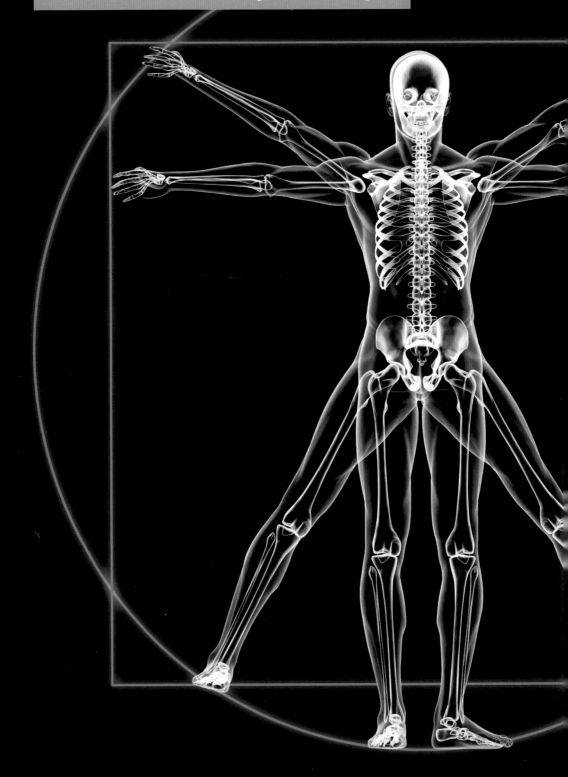

Human babies are born with about 300 bones. Adult humans have 206 bones. Some bones fuse together as humans grow.

THE HUMAN BODY

The human body is very strong in some ways. For example, a pumping heart can shoot blood nearly 10 metres (33 feet) from an open wound. The human body is also very weak at times. Human babies are born without the bones in their heads completely fused together. They can be easily injured.

Human bodies can be strange and surprising. Some people are double-jointed. They can stretch their joints more than most people. Other odd human traits involve the brain. Certain areas of the brain can fall asleep during the day. Other parts of the brain stay awake. Most people do not realize this is happening. They just go about their business as usual.

People do not agree about what human bodies can and cannot do. Not even scientists agree on everything. Scientists continue to research what is fact and what is fib about the human body. Some of what they have discovered may surprise you.

CHAPTER 1
HEADS AND BRAINS

The brain sends messages through the spinal column and other nerves that carry signals to the rest of the body.

Mammals are warm-blooded animals. Most mammals give birth to live babies. They do not lay eggs. Many newborn mammals can walk and feed themselves soon after they are born. This is not true for human babies. Humans develop survival skills over time. Many people believe it can take up to 18 years for children to be ready to live on their own. This is because human babies are born small, with undeveloped heads.

IT'S TRUE! Babies' brains are only 30 per cent of the size they will be when the baby grows up.

FACT OR FIB?

Human babies are born small, with undeveloped heads, because human mothers walk on two feet.

Evidence

Many **anthropologists** believe that a human mother's **pelvis** must remain small so she can walk upright on two feet. A small pelvis means a mother can only deliver a small baby.

A new study shows that there may be another reason. Researchers at the University of Rhode Island did a study. When a baby is inside the mother, it must get all of its energy from her. Just before the baby is born, it needs almost as much energy as the mother can make. The baby cannot stay inside the mother without hurting her.

Answer: UNDECIDED

A human baby's skull bones are not attached when it is born. This is an important clue. It means that a baby's head can change shape so that it can pass safely through the gap in the pelvis. There may also be other reasons that human babies are born so small. More studies are needed.

· ·

anthropologist scientist who studies human beings and human behaviour
pelvis wide, curved bones between the spine and the leg bones

How much of your brain do you use? Some people believe that they could do extraordinary things if only they could use all of their brain power.

FACT OR FIB?

Humans use only 10 per cent of their brain power.

Evidence

It is fun to think that humans could be smarter if only we could use our entire brains. Many people believe that not using all our brain power explains the genius of people like Einstein. He must have used more than 10 per cent of his brain.

Answer: FIB

We use all of our brains almost all of the time. Scientists have used imaging technology to show that human brains are active 24 hours a day. Many different regions of the brain work at the same time.

A neurologist is a doctor who treats people with brain disorders and problems with the nervous system.

IT'S TRUE!

The average human brain weighs about 1.4 kilograms (3 pounds). There is no relationship between brain size and intelligence. People with small brains and large brains have the same amount of intelligence.

CHAPTER 2

SIGHT

One of the most common eye disorders in children is amblyopia. This is sometimes called "lazy eye".

There is an urban legend that says that a baby's eye size does not change, even when the child grows. Urban legends are beliefs that people have even if there is often no evidence that they are true. For years, many new parents believed that almost everything about their baby would grow. The face, ears and nose would all get bigger. But they believed their baby's eyeballs would stay the same size.

IT'S TRUE!

Some people are colour-blind. This may mean that red and green look the same. It can also mean that they cannot see any colour at all. To these people the world appears in shades of grey, black and white.

FACT OR FIB?

Eyeballs stay the same size for a person's entire life.

Evidence

Experts know a lot about eyes. They understand why everyone is born with a lighter eye colour than they will have as adults. Eye experts also understand why some people cannot see very well. They use special tools to prescribe the right eyeglasses to people.

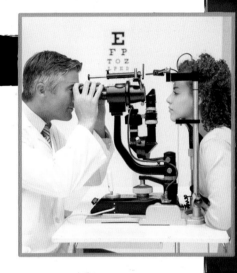

Answer: FIB

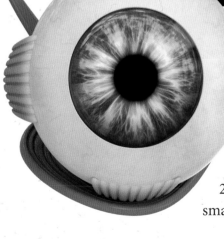

When babies are born, their eyeballs are about 75 per cent as big as they will one day be. Eye doctors report that the eyes grow quite a bit, especially in the first two years of life. Human eyes undergo another growth spurt during the teenage years.

An average adult eyeball is about 2.5 centimetres (1 inch) wide. That's a little smaller than the size of the average gumball.

CHAPTER 3

HEARING

Humans can hear more sounds than elephants, owls and goldfish. Humans do not hear as well as dogs, mice and rabbits.

Some people believe that what they eat can affect their hearing. Can salty foods make someone lose their hearing for a short amount of time?

What you eat can affect your hearing.

Evidence

Some studies show that overeating may make hearing more difficult. Some foods are thought to temporarily affect hearing. Salty foods can keep fluid in the body. When people have fluid in their ears, they may not hear as well.

IT'S TRUE! People with profound hearing loss can be helped by a **cochlear implant**. Unlike a hearing aid, which makes sounds louder, a cochlear implant stimulates the auditory nerve, which helps people to hear.

cochlear implant small electronic device that is surgically put into a person's head; cochlear implants allow sounds to get to the brain

Other foods may help hearing because they have **nutrients** that support better hearing. These foods include spinach, yoghurt, beans, tomatoes and nuts. Vitamin D, magnesium and folic acid are nutrients that support healthy hearing. Adding these nutrients to your diet may make a difference over time.

Answer: UNDECIDED

People who eat foods rich in potassium will find that the fluid and tissue in their ears is healthier. Foods with a lot of potassium include potatoes, bananas, yoghurt and milk. Experts note that eating good, nutritious foods will make all human bodies function better.

nutrient substance in foods that helps people grow, develop and stay healthy

CHAPTER 4
TASTE

Studies show that children love sour tastes more than adults do. That is one reason that sweets come in sour flavours.

Humans have five different tastes. These tastes are sweet, sour, salty, bitter and **umami**. *Umami* means "yummy" in Japanese. It is the flavour of meat stock.

The study of taste has changed over time. It used to be accepted that people tasted different flavours on different spots on their tongue. A "taste map" of the tongue was taught in schools. Scientists now know that every part of the tongue can sense all five tastes.

FACT OR FIB?

Humans taste only with their tongues.

Evidence

Many people believe that if a person has no sense of smell, they cannot taste. This condition is called anosmia. Studies show that people with anosmia can taste food. But the food tastes different to them than it does to others.

Answer: FIB

You cannot taste a thing with only your tongue. In order to taste, you also need saliva. Saliva is the liquid in your mouth. It breaks down food and separates the chemicals in the food. Receptors on the tongue are called taste buds. Taste buds find taste through food chemicals. Taste buds send messages to the brain through the nervous system.

IT'S TRUE!

By the time they're 60 years old, humans lose half of their taste buds.

umami rich taste that is commonly emphasized in Japanese foods, particularly kombu, a type of sea vegetable similar to kelp

CHAPTER 5

BONES

IT'S TRUE!

Humans have the same number of bones in their necks as giraffes do. The bones are simply smaller in humans!

People sometimes walk or talk in their sleep. But do they also grow in their sleep?

FACT OR FIB?

People are taller in the morning than they are at the end of the day.

Evidence

Humans have 33 **vertebrae**. These bones provide strength. They help people stand and walk upright. Our backbones let us turn and twist. They let us bend forwards and backwards. This is called flexibility. It allows the vertebrae to press together and stretch.

Answer: FACT

Studies show that people are about 0.25 cm (0.1 inch) taller when they wake up in the morning than they are at bedtime. This is because of your body weight. It causes your bones to get closer together while you stand all day. Lying down takes the weight off your back and allows it to stretch out at night.

As human bodies age, the change in the space between bones becomes permanent. People shrink, but do not regain their height overnight.

vertebrae small bones that are linked together to form the backbone

Cracking your knuckles makes a popping noise. It also causes temporary changes to the joints. Some people think this can cause permanent damage, such as **arthritis**. Osteoarthritis is the most common type of arthritis. It can be caused by wear and tear on the hands, finger joints, knees and hips.

FACT OR FIB?

Cracking your knuckles causes arthritis.

Some people crack their knuckles to relieve mental stress. Others find that their hands are more comfortable when they decompress their joints.

arthritis disease that causes swelling, stiffness and pain in a person's joints

Evidence

When you crack a joint, you stretch the joint capsule. A joint capsule protects the joint. It keeps the joint from moving in the wrong direction. When you stretch the joint capsule, gas is released. It forms bubbles and makes the popping sound you hear.

Answer: FIB

Studies show that people who crack their knuckles have the same chance of developing arthritis as those who do not crack their knuckles.

Dr Donald Unger wanted to study knuckle cracking. For 50 years he cracked the knuckles of his left hand twice a day. He did not crack the knuckles on his right hand. The knuckles on his left hand were cracked at least 36,500 times. The knuckles on his right hand were only cracked by accident. After 50 years of conducting his experiment, Unger did not have arthritis in either hand.

There is still a good reason to avoid the knuckle-cracking habit. Many people find the noise annoying. Also, people who crack their knuckles are more likely to have swollen hands.

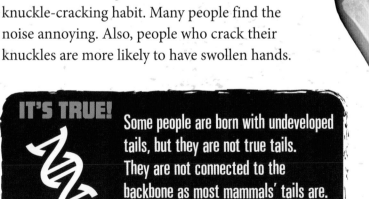

IT'S TRUE!
Some people are born with undeveloped tails, but they are not true tails. They are not connected to the backbone as most mammals' tails are.

CHAPTER 6

ORGANS

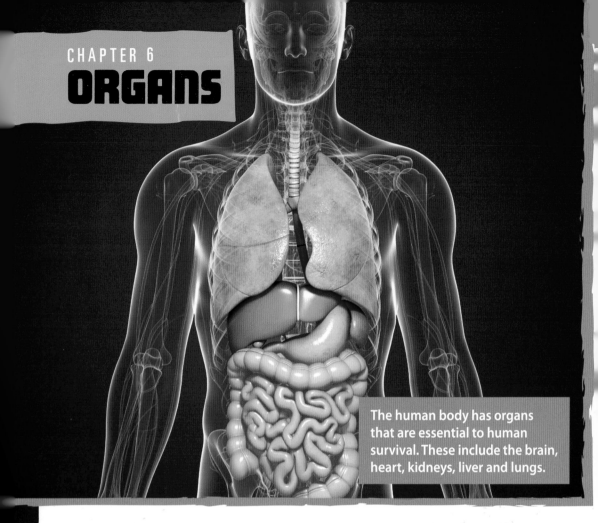

The human body has organs that are essential to human survival. These include the brain, heart, kidneys, liver and lungs.

The appendix is a small organ. It is finger-shaped. It is connected to the large intestine. When it hurts, you feel pain on the right-hand side of your belly. The word *appendix* comes from Latin. It means "an addition" or "something attached". Many people think the appendix is something that the body doesn't really need.

IT'S TRUE!

People with a hole in their heart should avoid SCUBA diving and travelling in outer space. The change in pressure could cause an air bubble to pass through the hole, which could be dangerous or even fatal.

FACT OR FIB?

Humans do not need an appendix.

Evidence

An appendectomy is an operation to remove an infected or swollen appendix. It is a common surgery. Every year, about 300,000 people have their appendix removed. Most people have no problems after the organ is removed. For years, scientists thought that humans had **evolved** to no longer need the appendix.

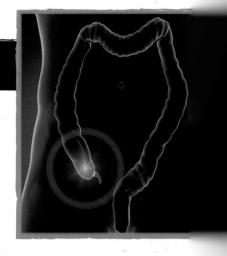

Answer: FIB

All humans are born with an appendix. Koalas and gorillas are also born with an appendix. Scientists have discovered that an appendix is important. It provides a safe place for good **bacteria** to grow. The digestive system uses good bacteria to help digest food. When a person gets ill, good bacteria can be killed off. The appendix holds good bacteria so that they can start to grow again once the person is healthy. This helps the digestive system.

evolve to develop gradually from a simple to complex form
bacteria tiny, single-celled organisms that can only be seen through a microscope; although some bacteria are harmful, many bacterial species are beneficial

When a starfish loses an arm, it will grow back. Some salamanders can grow back tails and organs. Rabbits can grow back parts of their earlobes. Bats can grow back parts of their wings. But can humans regrow damaged or lost body parts?

FACT OR FIB?

Humans can regrow body parts.

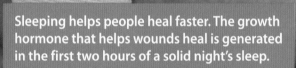

Sleeping helps people heal faster. The growth hormone that helps wounds heal is generated in the first two hours of a solid night's sleep.

Evidence

Human bodies often suffer injuries. The human body has developed many ways to heal and recover from wounds. Certain chemical reactions will stop a wound bleeding, and the body's **immune system** will help fight infection.

Answer: FIB

Human beings cannot regrow any part of their body except parts of their liver and skin. Experts do not understand why the liver regrows tissue. Scientists continue to research the liver. Sometimes a human organ, such as a heart or kidney, is diseased or damaged. It can be replaced. This operation is called a **transplant**. If a person loses an arm, leg, hand or foot, it can sometimes be reattached with surgery.

· ·

immune system network of cells, tissues and organs that work together to protect the body

transplant medical operation in which an organ or other part that has been removed from the body of one person is put into the body of another person

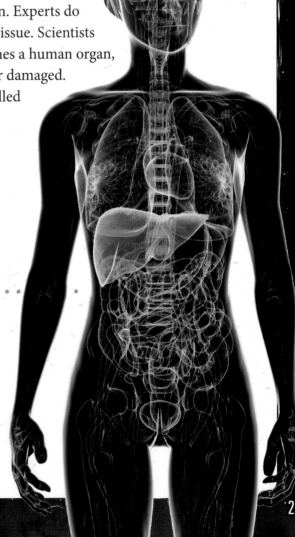

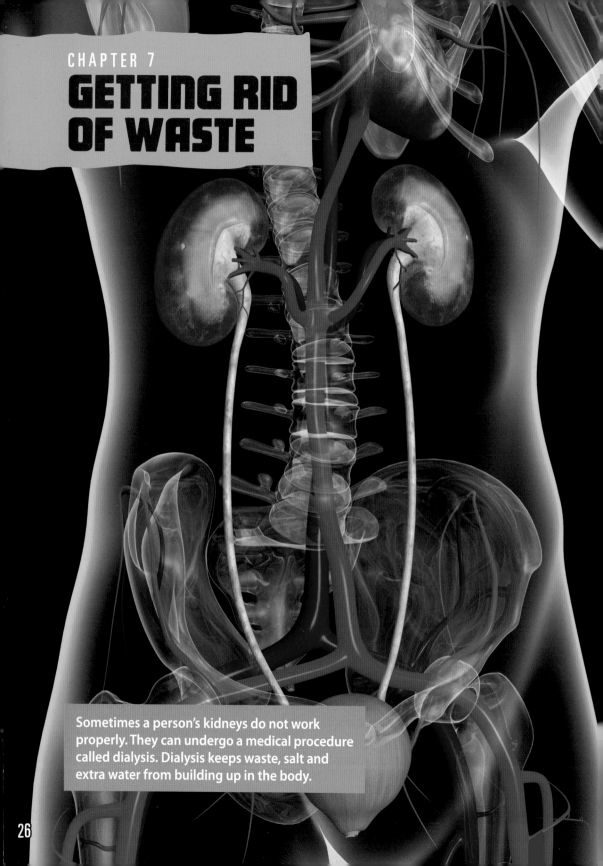

CHAPTER 7

GETTING RID OF WASTE

Sometimes a person's kidneys do not work properly. They can undergo a medical procedure called dialysis. Dialysis keeps waste, salt and extra water from building up in the body.

The human body has interesting ways of ridding itself of waste. Many people feel an urgent need to urinate in stressful situations. Urinating rids the body of waste. Others find that stress makes it so that they cannot urinate.

When the body is in a normal situation, the part of the brain called the **prefrontal cortex** makes decisions about going to the toilet. It usually follows the body's lead. When a person feels a sense of danger, the **limbic system** takes over. Sometimes people's bodies will not follow orders when it comes to going to the toilet. This is a result of what is called the "fight or flight" response. It protects people when they are in danger.

IT'S TRUE! Most animals and humans produce a chemical in their gall bladders that colours their droppings brown. Birds do not produce this chemical. That is why their droppings are mostly white.

prefrontal cortex part of the brain that plays an important role in what people think and do
limbic system part of the brain involved in emotional behaviour, fear and aggression

Breathing through your mouth will cause your bladder to shrink.

Evidence

When people feel they are in danger, they sometimes **hyperventilate**. This often means they breathe through the mouth. This has led to the idea that when people breathe through their mouths, their bladders shrink.

Answer: FIB

People may think that mouth-breathing is causing the bladder to shrink. However, some scientists believe this can be explained by other conditions. The fight or flight response might explain why people feel that they have to urinate more often when they hyperventilate.

Scientists have found that people who breathe through their mouths while sleeping sometimes have a condition called sleep apnoea. People with sleep apnoea stop breathing for certain amounts of time in their sleep. They also get up more to urinate in the night because their sleep is interrupted.

hyperventilate to breathe very quickly and deeply

Sneezing is an important part of the immune system. One sneeze can send 100,000 germs into the air.

IT'S TRUE!

People sneeze at about 161 kilometres (100 miles) per hour.

GLOSSARY

anthropologist scientist who studies human beings and human behaviour

arthritis disease that causes swelling, stiffness and pain in a person's joints

bacteria tiny, single-celled organisms that can only be seen through a microscope; although some bacteria are harmful, many bacterial species are beneficial

cochlear implant small electronic device that is surgically put into a person's head; cochlear implants allow sounds to get to the brain

evolve to develop gradually from a simple to complex form

hyperventilate to breathe very quickly and deeply

immune system network of cells, tissues and organs that work together to protect the body

limbic system part of the brain involved in emotional behaviour, fear and aggression

nutrient substance in foods that helps people grow, develop and stay healthy

pelvis wide, curved bones between the spine and the leg bones

prefrontal cortex part of the brain that plays an important role in what people think and do

transplant medical operation in which an organ or other part that has been removed from the body of one person is put into the body of another person

umami rich taste that is commonly emphasized in Japanese foods, particularly kombu, a type of sea vegetable similar to kelp

vertebrae small bones that are linked together to form the backbone

FIND OUT MORE

BOOKS

The Fact or Fiction Behind Human Bodies (Truth or Busted), Paul Mason (Wayland, 2014)

The Human Body (The World in Infographics), Jon Richards and Ed Simkins (Wayland, 2013)

Totally Wacky Facts About the Human Body (Mind Benders), Cari Meister (Capstone, 2016)

Utterly Amazing Human Body, Robert Winston (Dorling Kindersley, 2015)

WEBSITES

http://www.bbc.co.uk/education/topics/zcyycdm
Learn more about the human body and how it works.

https://www.natgeokids.com/uk/discover/science/general-science/15-facts-about-the-human-body/
Read facts about the human body.

https://www.dkfindout.com/uk/human-body/
Videos, diagrams and facts about the human body.

INDEX